THE 33 LAWS

OF

IMPACT & FULFILLMENT

THE 33 LAWS

OF

IMPACT & FULFILLMENT

Your Peak Performance Guide to
Leading from Within

MIKE DORSEY
"COACH MIKE D"

THE 33 LAWS OF IMPACT & FULFILLMENT

Your Peak Performance Guide to Leading from Within

GRATITUDE

First and foremost, I would like to thank God. I am a firm believer that everything good and perfect comes from above.

I would like to express my gratitude to the many individuals and communities who have supported me throughout my journey.

To my beloved wife Myisha, my children Morgan and Maxwell, my parents, my late grandparents, and my in-laws, thank you for your unwavering love and support. To my siblings, sisters-in-law, brother-in-law, uncles, aunts, cousins, God parents, God brothers, and God sisters, nieces, nephews, Godchildren, and friends, thank you for your presence in my life.

I also want to acknowledge the cities that have shaped me: Augusta Georgia, my birthplace, and Knoxville Tennessee, where (as an adult) I "grew up." To the countless individuals I have interviewed over the years and the countries and cities I've visited, thank you for sharing your stories and broadening my horizons.

To the organizations and educational institutions that have supported me, thank you for the opportunities to learn and grow. To my mentors, coaches, therapists, and all those who have offered guidance and support along the way, I am grateful for your wisdom and encouragement.

Finally, to the many individuals I have had the privilege of coaching, mentoring, and learning from, thank you for enriching my life and inspiring me to be my best self. In the words of the Swahili term Ubuntu, "I am because we are." To all of you, I say thank you.

CONTENTS

PRE-LAW
(INTRODUCTION)

WELCOME TO "THE 33 LAWS OF IMPACT & FULFILLMENT," a guidebook designed to help you reach your peak performance and lead from within. Whether you are a seasoned executive, a budding entrepreneur, or simply someone looking to make a meaningful difference in your life and career, this book offers valuable insights, tools, and strategies to help you unlock your full potential and live a life of purpose, impact, and fulfillment.

As someone who has coached and mentored countless individuals over the years, I have come to realize that many high-capacity individuals often settle for less than they are truly capable of achieving. This is often due to a lack of clarity, focus, or direction, coupled with a reluctance to step outside of their comfort zone and take risks. However, it doesn't have to be this way.

With the right mindset, habits, and actions, you can create the life and career you desire, one that aligns with your values and passions. But to do so, you need to embrace the power of self-awareness, goal-setting, communication, productivity, and leadership, which are the core themes that underpin the 33 laws of impact and fulfillment.

Throughout this book, I will guide you through each of these areas, offering practical advice and real-world examples that you can apply to your own life and career. From learning how to lean into your authentic truth and develop a growth mindset, to mastering the art of effective communication and building strong relationships, you will gain the knowledge and skills necessary to achieve your fullest potential and lead with impact.

One of the biggest challenges faced by individuals who elevate into leadership is disconnection. It's easy to lose touch with your roots and the people around you when you are busy climbing the corporate ladder or pursuing your entrepreneurial dreams. That's why I've included a stanza from one of my favorite poems, "If" by Rudyard Kipling, which exemplifies what true leadership is all about. "If you can talk with crowds and keep your virtue, Or walk with Kings—nor lose the common touch," It reminds us that we should be able to keep our virtues intact when amongst the crowds, yet not lose our common touch when around kings.

To be completely honest, seeking impact and fulfillment hit me on a much deeper level in 2016 while I was still in the pharmaceutical industry. I experienced two incidents that shook me to my core. One night, I woke up in a cold sweat with heart palpitations, feeling like I was having a heart attack. I managed to calm down and the symptoms eventually subsided. But not long after, the same thing happened again, and this time I was really scared. I went to the ER at 3am, where various machines were strapped to my body to determine what was going on. The diagnosis? Anxiety. It can feel and react in your body like a heart attack.

That wake-up call made me rethink the direction of my life. Despite having already launched a successful podcast and book, there was a deep-seated feeling of unfulfillment that kept me up at night. It was a nagging feeling that something was missing. When my company underwent a massive layoff not long after, I saw it as an opportunity to redirect my life. From that point forward, I was on a new mission to seek maximum impact and fulfillment in everything I do.

This book, "The 33 Laws of Impact & Fulfillment," is the result of my journey towards that mission.

So, if you're ready to maximize your impact and fulfillment, and live a life that truly matters, then this book is for you. I invite you to join me on this journey of self-discovery and growth, where we will explore the 33 laws of impact and fulfillment together and help you unlock your full potential. Let's do this together.

YOU ARE A 500-PIECE PUZZLE

WHEN I SPEAK AT VARIOUS EVENTS, I often use an icebreaker activity to engage the audience. One of my favorites is distributing a 500-piece puzzle to the crowd and allowing everyone to choose one piece each. After a few minutes, I ask them to write down what they think the puzzle looks like based on their one piece. Then, I divide them into small groups, and they compare and contrast their pieces before arriving at a collective guess of what the completed puzzle looks like. Finally, we reconvene as a larger group, and each small group shares their conclusions.

To date, not one person or group has been able to correctly identify the complete picture of the 500-piece puzzle. This activity serves as a powerful metaphor for how we view ourselves and others. We cannot define ourselves or others by any one piece, just as we cannot define a 500-piece puzzle by one piece. Moreover, it is incredibly difficult to understand ourselves or others when we only have a few pieces of information.

However, there is another side to this metaphor. Like a 500-piece puzzle, we are incomplete without all our pieces. We all have jagged and beautiful pieces, pieces we want to share with others and pieces we pray nobody finds out about. The unique thing about viewing ourselves as a puzzle is that we are not defined by any one piece, but we are also incomplete without all our pieces. Whether good, bad, or indifferent, all our pieces make up who we are.

Sometimes people define us by a single action, word, or achievement. They might view us through the lens of a monumental success or a devastating failure. However, we are not defined by any one of those pieces. It is important to acknowledge, accept, and come to terms with all our pieces. We should learn from them and accept them but not define ourselves by any singular piece.

On our journey of becoming the best version of ourselves, we should take an inventory of all our pieces. By acknowledging and accepting them, we can gain a better understanding of ourselves and others. We should also strive to see others as puzzles, understanding that we do not have all the pieces, and there is always more to learn. By doing so, we can cultivate empathy, compassion, and understanding, which are essential qualities for personal and collective growth.

In conclusion, the 500-piece puzzle activity serves as a powerful metaphor for understanding ourselves and others. We should strive to see ourselves and others as puzzles, acknowledging and accepting all our pieces, and not defining ourselves or others by any singular piece. By doing so, we can gain a deeper understanding of ourselves and others, and foster empathy, compassion, and growth.

MAKE THIS LAW PRACTICAL

Which pieces of my unique puzzle am I actively promoting, and which ones am I currently hiding? And why?

WISDOM + SELF CONTROL IS NECESSARY

IN TODAY'S FAST-PACED WORLD, it's easy to feel like we need to be constantly doing something. We're bombarded with messages telling us that we need to be productive all the time, that we need to be constantly working towards our goals. But is this really the best way to approach life? Is busyness always a sign of productivity, or is there more to it than that?

The truth is that without wisdom and self-control, abstaining from action may be the best policy. It's important to take a step back and really think about what we're doing and why we're doing it. Too often, we jump into things without any insight, without any direction, without any purpose, and without any self-control or wisdom to make proper decisions. This can lead to disaster.

Before taking action in a particular direction, we need to have an understanding of the triggers and influences in our lives that may have an impact on our level of self-control. We need to seek wisdom and have various frameworks in place to elicit self-control. Because a lot of times, we try things without these two components being present, and we're setting ourselves up for failure.

The concept of self-control is particularly important. It's not enough to simply have wisdom and insight into a situation. We need to be able to regulate our actions and make the right decisions even when things get tough. We need to be able to resist temptation and stay focused on our goals.

The problem is that so many of us have adopted a mindset of being busy. We think that being busy is synonymous with being productive. The more we do, the better we are. But this is a fallacy. As we grow older and gain more life experience, we come to realize that busyness does not equal productivity. In fact, it can often be the opposite.

Before taking action, it's important to pause and think about why we're doing what we're doing. Are we moving just to be moving, or do we have a clear purpose in mind? Do we have a plan in place to ensure that we stay on track and don't get sidetracked by distractions?

There are certainly times when it's important to take action and jump in with both feet. Sometimes, we need to build our wings on the way down. But even in these situations, it's important to have an understanding of who we are and what we're capable of. We need to know how to regulate the actions that we're going to take as there may be a component of wisdom embedded in the decision that we made to jump.

In any venture or action we take, wisdom and self-control are two friends that we would like to have along with us. These two components work hand-in-hand to ensure that we make the right decisions and stay on track towards our goals. Without them, we're likely to falter and fail.

So, the next time you're considering taking action, take a step back and really think about what you're doing. Seek wisdom and insight into the situation, and make sure that you have the self-control to follow through on your decisions. With these two friends by your side, you can be confident that you're making the right moves towards a more fulfilling life.

MAKE THIS LAW PRACTICAL

What areas of my life do I struggle with self-control the most, and how can I gain wisdom to improve in those areas? What are some sources I can tap into?

IT IS UNWISE TO OPERATE IN DOUBT

WHEN IT COMES TO MAKING IMPORTANT DECISIONS IN LIFE, doubt can be a formidable opponent. The fear of making the wrong move or taking a misstep can often hold us back from taking action. However, according to a good friend of mine, when in doubt, it's best to sit still. This simple yet profound statement has stuck with me for years, and it's a philosophy that I believe can be applied to many areas of life.

In our conversation about faith and direction, my friend shared with me his personal philosophy on decision-making. He said that when he is moved to take action, he does so with conviction and purpose. However, when he is not moved, he sits still and waits for the right moment to act. This approach is rooted in the belief that we should only move when we are truly motivated to do so.

As human beings, we are not perfect, and we will inevitably make mistakes. However, by moving only when we are truly inspired, we increase our chances of making the right decisions. Acting on impulse or without a clear sense of purpose can lead to unnecessary vulnerability and risk. Therefore, it's important to have faith and conviction in the moves that we make.

In fact, my friend Dr. Amos Johnson stated in a podcast episode that when we act in faith, we are not acting in sin. Conversely, when we act without faith, we are acting in doubt, which is synonymous with sin. This is an important point to consider when making decisions in life. Doubt can cloud our judgment and lead us down the wrong path. However, when we act with faith, we can be confident in our decisions and trust that we are on the right track.

This philosophy applies not only to major life decisions but also to everyday actions. For example, when I was playing football, I learned the importance of committing to my moves and making decisions with conviction. If I ran through a hole timidly, I was less likely to gain the necessary yardage. Additionally, I became more vulnerable to injury because I was not fully committed to my actions. On the other hand, when I acted with confidence and conviction, I was able to achieve my goals and avoid unnecessary risks.

Ultimately, the goal of any decision should be to maximize its impact while also leading us to fulfillment. When we act with faith and conviction, we increase our chances of achieving both. However, when we are in doubt, it's best to pause and wait for the right moment to act. Hesitation can create unnecessary vulnerability and lead to missed opportunities. Therefore, it's important to have a clear sense of purpose and motivation before making any move.

In conclusion, the philosophy of "when in doubt, sit still" is a powerful one that can help guide us in many areas of life. By acting with faith and conviction, we can make the right decisions and achieve our goals. However, when we are in doubt, it's important to take a step back and wait for the right moment to act. This approach can help us avoid unnecessary risks and ensure that our actions are motivated by a clear sense of purpose.

MAKE THIS LAW PRACTICAL

Has doubting myself ever led to a significant achievement?
When was the last time doubt played a role in my success?

IMPACT + FULFILLMENT IS A PRIORITY

THE OBJECTIVE OF THIS PROJECT is to assist you in achieving your full potential and satisfaction in life. I believe that every individual has a natural desire and goal to do so. However, when we talk about impact and fulfillment, we need to understand what they mean. While dictionaries may provide differing definitions, we will create our own definitions to help you unlock and become the best version of yourself.

In my opinion, impact refers to the change or difference associated with your involvement. This can be positive or negative. When it comes to professional pursuits or business endeavors, we tend to focus on revenue, number of customers, or reviews. These are indicators of your impact, and if they are decreasing, it could mean that your involvement is not having a positive effect. It is important to recognize that we may not be exceptional in every situation, but the ultimate goal is to assess our gifts, talents, skills, and relationships and find a way to optimize them towards making positive change. This is the essence of impact.

On the other hand, fulfillment is related to your core beliefs, joy, purpose, and why. It involves tapping into your true essence. When someone is fulfilled, they are content and aligned with their purpose, without being complacent. They strive to improve and become better because they are confident that they are on the right path. Fulfillment is the through line to your beliefs, purpose, and why. When you optimize your fulfillment in life, you experience a level of peace that enables you to make clearer decisions.

While everything may not be perfect, the ultimate goal is to align yourself with opportunities, relationships, and circumstances that provide you with the maximum capacity for optimized impact and fulfillment. This requires a deep dive into who you are and an honest assessment of your gifts and talents. When you can tap into your true essence, you can optimize your impact and fulfillment in life.

To achieve this, start by identifying your core beliefs, joy, purpose, and why. What are the things that you are truly passionate about? What are the things that bring you contentment? How can you align your gifts and talents with your purpose? Once you have a clear understanding of this, you can start identifying opportunities and relationships that align with your purpose and help you achieve your goals.

It is important to recognize that optimizing your impact and fulfillment may require you to step outside of your comfort zone. It may require you to take risks and make difficult decisions. However, when you are aligned with your purpose, you will have the confidence to take on new challenges and pursue opportunities that may have seemed impossible before.

In conclusion, optimizing your impact and fulfillment in life requires a deep understanding of who you are and what you are truly passionate about. By aligning your gifts and talents with your purpose, you can make a positive impact and experience a level of fulfillment that will enable you to make clearer decisions and pursue new opportunities with confidence. Remember, everything may not be perfect, but the ultimate goal is to align yourself with circumstances that provide you with the maximum capacity for optimized impact and fulfillment.

MAKE THIS LAW PRACTICAL:

How do you define living a fulfilling and impactful life based on your personal beliefs, interests, and circumstances?

VALUE SUPERSEDES COST

IF YOU WERE TO ASK ANYONE in my circle of friends, they would probably describe me as being "economical" - a polite way of saying that I'm cheap. And to be honest, I do have issues with spending money, especially on things that I don't value. If I don't see the value in something, I have a hard time justifying the cost.

But it's not that I'm cheap in general - it's just that I'm selective about where I put my money. For example, my wife and I really enjoy good food, so we don't hesitate to spend a couple hundred dollars on a nice meal for date night. But I wouldn't spend that kind of money on a pair of sneakers.

The key here is value. I value experiences over material possessions, so I'm willing to spend money on things that will provide me with a valuable experience. On the other hand, I don't see the value in owning expensive things just for the sake of having them.

When it comes to cost, I do consider it, but it's not my primary focus. Instead, I'm more concerned with the value that something will provide me. If I see the value in something, I'm willing to pay a premium for it. But if there's no value, then I won't spend a penny.

This mindset is important to keep in mind when making purchasing decisions. It's easy to get caught up in the cost of something and forget to consider the value. But if we want to be mindful with our money, we need to focus on the value and whether it aligns with our priorities.

It's also important to recognize that value is subjective. What one person finds valuable might not be valuable to someone else. That's why it's essential to know yourself and your priorities before making purchasing decisions.

In the end, it's not about being cheap or spending money frivolously. It's about being intentional with our money and using it in a way that aligns with our values and priorities. So the next time you're considering a purchase, ask yourself: does this align with my values? Does it provide me with value? If the answer is yes, then it's worth considering the cost.

MAKE THIS LAW PRACTICAL

What tangible things and experiences do you value the most?
Take an inventory of how you spend your time and money.
Are you allocating your time and resources towards the things
and experiences you value most? If not, why not?

TUBE CAPACITY > VESSEL CAPACITY

WHEN WE ARE IN A POSITION OF LEARNING, we often adopt the mindset of becoming a vessel. We see ourselves as containers, soaking up all the wisdom that others can pour into us. This perspective is often praised and encouraged, and it can be found in various religious texts. However, I challenge this perspective. I have come to understand that the most influential individuals in the world do not live their lives as vessels; they operate as tubes.

There is a crucial difference between a vessel and a tube. A vessel is a container that gets filled up, but the contents of that vessel are not necessarily beneficial to anyone else unless the vessel leaks, breaks, or spills over. On the other hand, a tube allows whatever comes in one side to flow out the other. It is a conduit for information, knowledge, and wisdom, and it is meant to be shared with others.

When we operate as tubes, we have the perspective that what comes into us is not necessarily for us to keep but for us to let flow through to the people who need it most. We become the conduit for the wisdom and knowledge that we have acquired, and our focus shifts from ourselves to others. We start to impact people on a very deep level, and we operate at a very high level.

Operating as a tube requires unwavering belief and faith that the source of the information or knowledge that flows into us will not be shut off. We must believe that the faucet will keep flowing, and we must trust that what comes to us is meant to flow through us. We become fortified by the information that flows through us, and our faith strengthens us.

If you are not yet ready to operate as a tube, that is okay. Continue to be a vessel until you feel ready to morph into a tube. Once you are walking in your purpose and living a life of maximum impact and fulfillment, you will naturally shift from being a vessel to becoming a tube.

In conclusion, the goal is to be a tube, not a vessel. As a tube, we become conduits for wisdom, knowledge, and information. We impact people on a deep level, and we operate at a high level. We trust that the information that flows into us will keep flowing, and we become fortified by the knowledge that flows through us. So look in the mirror and decide whether you have enough faith to operate as a tube. If you do, your life will be transformed, and you will impact the world in ways that you never thought possible.

MAKE THIS LAW PRACTICAL

What things or beliefs are you currently holding onto that you know deep down are not meant for you to keep?

TRUTH AND LOVE ARE NECESSARY FOR EFFECTIVE COMMUNICATION

IN A SERMON A FEW YEARS AGO, my former pastor and good friend, Pastor Derick Wakefield, shared a powerful message that resonates deeply with me. He said, "Love without truth is hypocrisy, and truth without love is brutality." This statement is one that we should all take to heart because it speaks to the im-portance of both love and truth in our interactions with others.

We have all encountered people who claim to love us, but their actions and words do not align with that love. This is what Pastor Wakefield meant when he said, "Love without truth is hypocrisy." If you truly love someone, you must be honest with them, even when it is difficult. Love that is not grounded in truth is not genuine and can lead to misunderstandings, hurt feelings, and broken relationships.

On the other hand, we have also encountered people who are brutally honest, using truth as a weapon to hurt others. This is what Pastor Wakefield meant when he said, "Truth without love is brutality." While it is important to be direct in our communication, we must also be mindful of the impact our words can have on others. We should always try to communicate with love and empathy, even when we are delivering difficult truths.

When we communicate with both love and truth, we have the potential to accomplish great things. By being honest with others and expressing our love and care for them, we can build strong relationships that stand the test of time. On the other hand, when we communicate harshly or dishonestly, we risk damaging those relationships and causing harm to others.

Ultimately, our goal should be to help people and make a positive impact in the world. When we approach life with the mindset of both love and truth, we have the potential to do just that. By communicating honestly and empathetic with others, we can build trust and understanding. And when we act with love and care for those around us, we can create a better world for everyone.

In conclusion, the message of "Love without truth is hypocrisy, and truth without love is brutality" is one that we should all take to heart. By striving to communicate with both love and truth, we can build strong relationships and make a positive impact in the world. Let us all strive to live our lives in this way, with a commitment to both love and truth in all that we do.

MAKE THIS LAW PRACTICAL

Can you recall a time when being brutally honest has served you well in the past? If so, how? On the flip side, have you ever felt love and support from someone who was not entirely truthful with you? If yes, please explain.

8ᵀᴴ LAW

PRIORITIZE "THE RIGHT ONES"

THE ESSENCE OF THIS LAW can be summed up in one phrase: prioritize the right ones. The ones who possess the qualities necessary to lead with a focus on the collective good rather than their own individual success. For far too long, the wrong ones have been occupying positions of power and influence, leading to a trickle-down economic theory that benefits only a select few. It's time to shift our priorities and ensure that the right ones win and win big because when they do, we all win.

As we move through life and ascend into positions of influence, it's important to remember that our impact on humanity will continue long after we're gone. How will we leave this world in a better position than we found it? This question is central to determining whether we are one of the right ones. If we prioritize creating opportunities for others and making things better, we might be on the right track. However, if we conduct our lives through a selfish lens, solely focused on our own acquisition and hoarding of resources, we might need to shift our philosophy and mindset.

The right ones possess a unique set of qualities that distinguish them from the wrong ones. They lead with empathy, prioritizing the needs of the collective over their own self-interest. They possess a vision for a better future and have the courage to pursue it relentlessly. They inspire and empower others to achieve their full potential, creating a ripple effect that extends far beyond their immediate sphere of influence.

It's crucial to prioritize the right ones because they hold the key to unlocking the greatest potential for humanity. When we put them in positions of power and influence, we create opportunities that spill over to benefit a greater number of individuals and society as a whole. This is in stark contrast to the trickle-down economic theory that has been perpetuated by the wrong ones for far too long, leaving most people behind.

As we work to prioritize the right ones, it's important to recognize that this is a collective effort. We all have a role to play in identifying and supporting those who possess the qualities necessary to lead with a focus on the collective good. This requires a shift in mindset and a commitment to creating a better future for all.

In conclusion, prioritizing the right ones is essential to unlocking the greatest potential for humanity. We need to shift our priorities and ensure that those who lead with empathy, vision, and the ability to inspire and empower others are the ones occupying positions of power and influence. This requires a collective effort and a commitment to creating a better future for all.

MAKE THIS LAW PRACTICAL

Create a list of individuals, organizations, and institutions that you believe are doing meaningful work and making a positive impact. How do you plan to support them and contribute to their growth and success?

EMBRACE "THE ORIGINAL TRUTH" ABOUT YOU

THE PURSUIT OF PERSONAL GROWTH and development is a journey that can lead to the discovery of our original truth. Dr. Myles Munroe, in one of his sermons, stated that the original truth about us will shock us and amaze everyone else. This statement holds true for many individuals who have embarked on the path of self-discovery and understanding their purpose, gifts, talents, and skills.

Many of us tend to sleepwalk through life, following the path that was laid out for us by someone else. We may find some fulfillment in that path, but we often wake up feeling like something is not adding up. The reason for this is that we may not be embracing our original truth. Once we come to grips with our original truth, it's like a light shines, and we awaken to a new reality.

For the late Dr. Myles Munroe, understanding his original truth was a transformative experience. It awakened something inside of him that wouldn't let him rest until he began operating within that gift. Once he embraced his purpose of encouraging, empowering, and enhancing individuals to maximum impact and fulfillment, he found a sense of peace and contentment that he couldn't achieve before.

Living life while embracing our original truth is crucial to our overall well-being. It doesn't matter whether it's our job, business, or vocation; our original truth should always shine. We were put on this planet to live our original truth, and when we do, we feel alive.

Unfortunately, many of us live life with a mask on, playing a character to fit in with others. But the moment we wake up to our original truth, we start living a life that is authentic and fulfilling. We become a magnet for others who are also on the same journey of self-discovery.

Discovering our original truth requires deep introspection and a willingness to peel back the layers that we've built up over the years. It may take time, but it's worth it. Once we understand our original truth, we can start living a life that aligns with our purpose and brings us the greatest joy and fulfillment.

Living a life while embracing our original truth is not always easy. We may face challenges and obstacles that test our resolve. But when we stay true to ourselves and our purpose, we can overcome any obstacle that comes our way.

In conclusion, embracing our original truth is crucial to our overall well-being and happiness. It requires us to do the deep work of self-discovery and understand our purpose, gifts, talents, and skills. Once we come to grips with our original truth, we awaken to a new reality that is authentic and fulfilling. So, let us all commit to living a life while embracing our original truth, and we will amaze everyone we encounter.

MAKE THIS LAW PRACTICAL

What is your original truth? How do you plan to honor and uphold it in your life, and what actions will you take to align your decisions and actions with this truth?

GRASP THE FRAMEWORK THAT MOTIVATES YOU

As a coach who has worked with individuals from different walks of life, I have come to realize that people tend to fall into one of two categories: task masters or directionally driven individuals. Task masters are those who are motivated by achieving specific goals and tend to set small, medium, and long-term objectives to fulfill their purpose. They feel fulfilled once they accomplish a task, but often struggle when they don't have another goal to work towards. On the other hand, directionally driven individuals are not always motivated by completing goals and tasks but by being in the right direction and alignment with their passions and purpose.

If you're a task master, you may find yourself motivated by having a clear goal to work towards and a sense of accomplishment once you achieve it. However, you may also find it challenging to stay motivated when you don't have a specific goal to work on. In contrast, if you're directionally driven, you may feel restricted and frustrated when given a direct path to a particular task or goal. You may be someone who prefers ambiguity and flexibility, and you feel energized when given the opportunity to be creative and use your gifts, talents, and skills.

Understanding your personal wiring is crucial because it helps you construct the right framework to make the maximum impact, you're capable of while also gaining fulfillment in your activities. There is no right or wrong way to be, but the key is to be in alignment with who you are, rather than forcing yourself down a path that is not congruent with your nature.

If you're unsure about which category you fall into, take a moment to reflect on what motivates you and what makes you feel fulfilled. Do you thrive on completing tasks and accomplishing goals, or do you prefer to be in alignment with your passions and purpose? Once you have a better understanding of your personal wiring, you can create a framework that aligns with your nature and maximizes your impact.

For task masters, creating a list of short-term and long-term goals may be helpful. You may also benefit from breaking down larger goals into smaller, more manageable tasks to keep yourself motivated. If you find yourself feeling unfulfilled once a task is complete, try setting a new goal or finding a new challenge to work towards.

For directionally driven individuals, focusing on your passions and purpose may be more beneficial. You may find that working on projects that align with your values and interests is more fulfilling than working on specific tasks or goals. However, it's important to balance your desire for creativity and flexibility with the need for structure and accountability to ensure that you're making progress towards your overall vision.

In conclusion, whether you're a task master or directionally driven, understanding your personal wiring is essential for creating a framework that aligns with your nature and maximizes your impact. Take the time to reflect on what motivates you and what makes you feel fulfilled and use that information to create a plan that works for you. Remember, there is no right or wrong way to be, the only wrong way is to force yourself down a path that is not congruent with who you are.

MAKE THIS LAW PRACTICAL

Are you directionally driven, a task master or a hybrid of both? What category do the individuals and teams you lead fall into? With this clarity, how will your strategic planning and goal setting be impacted?

SPEND SIGNIFICANT TIME WITH YOURSELF

BEING ALONE AND SPENDING TIME WITH ONESELF are two different things. It is possible to be alone and not present, not paying attention to oneself, or one's surroundings. Just like being with another person, being alone does not necessarily mean one is spending quality time with oneself. It is crucial to spend quality time with oneself, to learn about oneself, to understand oneself, and to optimize one's potential.

When we spend time with ourselves, we start to learn about ourselves. We begin to understand what makes us tick, what makes us feel a certain way, what causes us to have certain reactions, and what causes us to respond in a particular way. We start to pay attention to the nuances of what's happening in our minds and bodies. We start to understand why our heart rate goes up or why we feel calm in certain environments. We start to pay attention to our thoughts, emotions, and physical sensations. This self-awareness is essential to fully understand ourselves and to optimize our potential.

When we don't spend quality time with ourselves, we miss out on important information about ourselves. We may not realize what is causing us stress or what is triggering our anxiety. We may not notice patterns in our behavior or habits. We may not be aware of our strengths or weaknesses. This lack of self-awareness can limit our ability to grow and develop as individuals.

Furthermore, spending time with ourselves shows that we matter to ourselves. When we take the time to learn about ourselves, we show ourselves that we are important. We start to prioritize our needs and desires. We begin to make choices that align with our values and beliefs. This self-love and self-care can lead to increased self-esteem and confidence.

It is important to note that being alone does not necessarily mean we are lonely. Loneliness is a feeling of isolation or disconnectedness, while being alone can be a choice. Some people enjoy spending time alone and find it rejuvenating. However, even those who prefer to be alone can benefit from spending quality time with themselves.

For example, I recently discovered that I am an ambivert. I am an introvert who is good with people and can perform in front of crowds. However, I also value my alone time and need decompression time after being in social situations. Through spending time with myself, I learned that I do not necessarily need crowds to have a good time. This self-awareness has helped me make choices that align with my needs and desires.

Self-awareness can also help us navigate challenging situations. When we understand our triggers and reactions, we can better manage our emotions and responses. We can make choices that align with our values and beliefs. For example, if we know that certain situations or people trigger our anxiety, we can prepare ourselves by practicing self-care and setting boundaries.

In conclusion, being alone and spending quality time with oneself are two different things. While it is possible to be alone and not present, spending quality time with oneself can lead to increased self-awareness, self-love, and self-care. It can help us understand our triggers, reactions, strengths, and weaknesses. It can also help us navigate challenging situations and make choices that align with our values and beliefs. So, if you want to optimize your impact and fulfillment, start by spending quality time with yourself. Pay attention, learn something, and then you can grow and build.

MAKE THIS LAW PRACTICAL

What are the issues and challenges that I struggle with that make it difficult for me to "spend time with myself?" Are there things that a licensed therapist could help me unpack and gain clarity on? If so, when will I explore making an appointment to see a therapist?

OPEN SOURCE YOUR LEARNING AND CLOSELY GUARD YOUR COUNSEL

IN TODAY'S SOCIETY, we have access to an unprecedented amount of information. From news articles to documentaries to personal stories shared online, we can learn about any topic we desire with just a few clicks. It's important to take advantage of this wealth of knowledge, to open source our learning and gain as much insight and understanding as possible. However, while we can freely access information, we must guard our counsel closely.

Why is it necessary to guard our counsel? Information is generic; it is not tailored to our personal experience. Therefore, it is important to think about information through a contextual lens, as this will determine how we apply the knowledge we've gained. The way we contextualize information will impact the actions we take. It's essential to be mindful of who we allow to counsel us, as we are opening ourselves up to taking advice and potentially acting on it.

Vetting those we allow to counsel us is crucial, as they can lead us down the wrong path. When we put ourselves in a position to take action, we need to be sure that the individual we are seeking counsel from is trustworthy and respectful. They should have some level of relationship or trust with us, as they will have direct access to the things that drive us. Just as we wouldn't invite a stranger into our home to interact with our family without proper vetting, we should be cautious about who we allow into our mindset, spirit, and thought process.

Closely guarding our counsel is as vital as opening ourselves up to learning and gathering information. When we allow someone to counsel us, we are potentially taking action based on their advice. In contrast, acquiring information is simply acquiring data. The actions we take based on counsel can have a significant impact on our lives, so it's essential to be cautious and ensure that the advice we receive aligns with our values and beliefs.

To maximize our impact and optimize our fulfillment in life, we need to strike a balance between open sourcing our learning and guarding our counsel. It's important to be open to new ideas and perspectives while also ensuring that those we allow to counsel us have our best interests in mind. By doing so, we can contextualize the information we acquire and use it to make informed decisions that align with our values and beliefs.

In conclusion, in today's world, we have access to a wealth of information. It's important to take advantage of this and open source our learning to gain as much insight and understanding as possible. However, we must also be cautious about who we allow to counsel us. By doing so, we can contextualize the information we acquire and make informed decisions that align with our values and beliefs. By striking a balance between open sourcing our learning and guarding our counsel, we can maximize our impact and optimize our fulfillment in life.

MAKE THIS LAW PRACTICAL

Who are my trusted advisors? Why do I trust their advice and counsel?

EMBRACE ONE MOMENT AT A TIME

As HUMAN BEINGS, we often get caught up in the idea of time. We think about the past and reminisce about memories we have already made. We worry about the future and what it might hold. Rarely do we focus on the present moment, the only moment that truly exists. When someone asks us how we're doing, we might respond with "fine" or "good," but do we ever stop to truly reflect on how we are feeling in that very moment?

This is where the concept of living one moment at a time comes in. It's not about living one day at a time or even one week at a time. It's about being present in the moment and fully experiencing it. When we live one moment at a time, we can break down our day into smaller, more manageable pieces. If we focus on having a great moment, we can use it as inspiration to continue with the rest of our day. On the other hand, if we're having a bad moment, we can be confident that it will pass and not let it spoil the rest of our day.

We often think that time can be sped up or slowed down, but in reality, time is constant. We can't control it, but we can control how we experience it. By being fully present in the moment, we can minimize distractions and truly live in the present. When we do this, we might even feel like time is slowing down, but in reality, we're just making the most of the time we have.

Living one moment at a time requires us to be intentional about our thoughts and actions. It means being mindful of our surroundings and the people we interact with. When we live one moment at a time, we have the capacity to maximize our impact and fulfillment. We can make the most of each moment, and in doing so, we can live a more meaningful and fulfilling life.

This mindset can be especially helpful in times of stress or uncertainty. When we're overwhelmed, it's easy to get caught up in the future and worry about what might happen. By focusing on one moment at a time, we can reduce anxiety and bring ourselves back to the present moment. It allows us to take things one step at a time and not get overwhelmed by the bigger picture.

Living one moment at a time is not always easy. We live in a fast-paced world, and it's easy to get caught up in the hustle and bustle of everyday life. But by taking a step back and focusing on the present moment, we can live a more mindful and intentional life. It's not about living one day at a time or even one week at a time, but rather living in the moment and fully experiencing each and every one. By doing so, we can maximize our impact and fulfillment and truly live a life worth living.

MAKE THIS LAW PRACTICAL

What are some practices that I will commit to incorporating that will allow me to be more present in the moment?

LEARN WITH INTENTION

LEARNING IS A LIFELONG PROCESS, and the opportunities to gain knowledge, experience, and wisdom are endless. However, it's not just about accumulating information but also about how we apply it to our lives and help others do the same. Therefore, it's essential to learn with the intention of living and make the most of the knowledge we acquire.

The purpose of learning is to gain practical insight that helps us live better and serve others. We should strive to restructure our framework around learning and approach it with intentionality. The goal is to step into situations and learn something that benefits us or others, serving as a conduit for the flow of information, knowledge, and wisdom to those in need. The aim is not to be in perpetual learning but to learn so that we can live a fulfilling life.

A lot of people have the wrong perspective when it comes to learning. They think of it as something that fills their brains with random knowledge or information. However, the real goal of learning is to gain practical insights that will help us live a better life. We should approach learning with the mindset of applying what we learn and sharing it with those who need it. This is where the true value of learning lies.

For example, if we go to the gym, our goal should not be to train harder just for the sake of it. Instead, we should train hard so that we can live a better life outside the gym. We should approach learning the same way, with the intention of applying what we learn to improve our lives and help others do the same.

Learning with the intention of living means that we are intentional about the information, knowledge, and wisdom we acquire. We consider how we can apply it to our lives and how we can use it to benefit others. This mindset allows us to live a life that is both fulfilling and impactful.

Furthermore, our ultimate goal should be to help others live better as well. We should not only focus on our own growth and development but also on how we can serve others. When we learn something new, we should ask ourselves how we can use that knowledge to help someone else. This approach will allow us to have maximum impact and fulfillment.

In conclusion, learning is a lifelong process that should be approached with intentionality. We should not just accumulate knowledge but also apply it to our lives and share it with those who need it. The ultimate goal should be to live a fulfilling life and help others do the same. By adopting this mindset, we can make the most of every learning opportunity and have a meaningful impact on the world.

MAKE THIS LAW PRACTICAL:

What is one new thing I've learned that I can implement today, and how can I speed up my learning process to maximize my time practicing what I've learned?

FEED THE CURIOSITY WITHIN

AS A CHILD, I was taught that being a jack of all trades is not desirable, and that it's better to specialize in one area to become a master. However, I recently stumbled upon another interpretation that supposedly was in reference to William Shakespeare that says, "a jack of all trades is a master of none, but oftentimes better than a master of one." This changed my perspective on the matter, and I realized that the quote was actually a compliment to those who have a diverse set of skills and interests.

Many parents and educators try to push children towards specializing in one area. While this approach may work for some, there are many individuals whose strengths lie in their diverse perspectives and broad range of interests. These individuals possess a unique ability to draw upon multiple skill sets and combine them in creative ways due to their curiosity and broad bank of knowledge. As adults, it's important to recognize and embrace these strengths. If you're someone with a diverse skill set and interests, don't feel like you have to conform to the idea of being a master in one area. Your strengths may lie in your ability to be a jack of all trades, and that could be your superpower.

It's crucial to understand and accept ourselves for who we are, and to not try to be someone we're not. Comparison is often the thief of joy, and trying to become someone we are not can lead to feelings of inadequacy and dissatisfaction. We need to identify our unique strengths and abilities and focus on becoming the best version of ourselves. This is where we'll find the most impact and fulfillment.

The full quote in reference to Shakespeare reminds us that being a jack of all trades is not necessarily a bad thing. In fact, it can be a valuable asset. Having a broad range of knowledge and skills allows us to see things from different perspectives and approach problems in innovative ways. It's important to embrace and develop our diverse skill sets, rather than feeling like we have to specialize in one area to be successful.

In conclusion, the idea that being a jack of all trades is a negative trait is a misconception. The full quote highlights the value of having a diverse set of skills and interests. It's important to embrace and develop our unique strengths, rather than trying to conform to society's expectations. By doing so, we can unleash our full potential and make a meaningful impact in the world.

MAKE THIS LAW PRACTICAL:

In what areas of my life has my curiosity led me to have a broad understanding of various subject matters?

STRENGTHEN THE INTANGIBLES BEFORE EMBRACING THE TACTICAL

IN THE PURSUIT OF SUCCESS, we often find ourselves searching for the perfect plan. We seek out gurus, experts, and key opinion leaders in the hope of discovering the secret to reaching the Promised Land. We believe that if we can just find that one golden nugget, success will be within our grasp. However, what we fail to realize is that success is not solely dependent on a flawless plan. An impeccable plan, in the hands of an incapable man or woman, is meaningless.

When we sit down with successful individuals, we often expect to hear about some groundbreaking secret to their success. Yet, what we come to realize is that there are very few secrets in life that lead to success. Most successful individuals simply excel at doing what they do best, and they do it consistently. By staying focused on their unique strengths, talents, and skills, they are able to achieve monumental levels of success.

While it may be tempting to try and replicate the success of others by adopting their plans, this approach is not foolproof. The reason for this is that success is not solely dependent on a plan, but also on the individual's alignment with that plan. A great plan in the wrong hands will not lead to success. Therefore, it is crucial to begin with the internal work of identifying your own unique strengths, gifts, talents, and skills. Only then can you pursue plans that are in alignment with your skill set and set yourself up for monumental success.

It is essential to recognize that success is not a one-size-fits-all approach. What works for one individual may not work for another. The key is to find what works for you and stay committed to it. This involves doing the necessary internal work to identify your unique strengths and capabilities. Once you have done so, you can begin to craft a plan that aligns with your strengths and abilities, setting you up for success.

The journey to success requires more than just a flawless plan. It requires a commitment to personal growth and self-discovery. When we take the time to do the internal work, we gain a better understanding of ourselves, our strengths, and our limitations. Armed with this knowledge, we are better equipped to navigate the challenges that come our way and capitalize on our strengths to achieve monumental success.

In conclusion, an impeccable plan alone is not enough to guarantee success. It is essential to do the internal work of identifying your unique strengths, talents, and skills before embarking on any external plan. Success is not a one-size-fits-all approach, and what works for one individual may not work for another. By staying focused on your strengths and abilities, you can craft a plan that aligns with your unique skill set and set yourself up for monumental success. Remember, success is not just about having a flawless plan, but also about being the right person to execute it.

MAKE THIS LAW PRACTICAL

What personal growth is necessary for me to achieve my goals?

START WITH "I AM"

THE I AM FOUNDATION is a building built on the belief that anything that starts with "I am" is an acknowledgement that one owns and understands what is being described. This Foundation is built on seven core pillars, which include belief systems, integrity, decision making, intention and openness, growth, resource management, and sustainability.

Belief systems are the first pillar and involve understanding what one believes in, why they believe it, how they practice and reinforce that belief, and how they put it to the test. Believing in something bigger than oneself is the core of the I Am Foundation.

Integrity is the second pillar and involves one's word being their bond. What one stands on is their word, and their integrity is key. The root to the I Am Foundation lies in integrity.

Decision making is the third pillar and requires individuals to make decisions regularly. The types of decisions made can be up for debate, but the impact of those decisions is undeniable. The decisions one makes today can impact their life and the lives of those connected to them.

The fourth pillar is intention and openness, which require direction and a focus on movement. Staying open to opportunities is also essential as it allows one to become the best version of themselves. Being intentional and open at the same time is essential to achieving one's goals.

Growth is the fifth pillar, and it involves becoming more of who one is by growing in their belief systems, integrity, decision making, intention and openness. Growth is essential for anyone looking to build a solid foundation.

Resource management is the sixth pillar and involves managing the resources one has at their disposal effectively. Resources can include skills, talents, financial resources, and teams. Learning how to manage these resources properly allows one to become a good steward of their gifts.

The last pillar is sustainability, which involves putting systems in place to maintain and cultivate more of who one is. We are meant to grow, develop, and evolve, and sustainability helps us do just that. The systems put in place should help us maintain and grow into the best version of ourselves.

The I Am Foundation is built on these core pillars, and they are all interconnected. Belief systems lead to integrity, which leads to better decision making. Intention and openness lead to growth, which leads to better resource management, which ultimately leads to sustainability.

The I Am Foundation is a reminder that everything starts with oneself. It is a reminder that we are responsible for who we are and what we become. The Foundation encourages individuals to take ownership of their lives and become the best version of themselves.

MAKE THIS LAW PRACTICAL

Using the components of the 'I AM Foundation', create my personal 'I AM' Foundation.

HALL OF FAME PLAYERS RARELY BECOME HALL OF FAME COACHES

HALL OF FAME PLAYERS AND HALL OF FAME COACHES are two distinct categories in sports. While there are some coaches who were also great players in their prime, it is rare to find individuals who excel in both roles. This is because being a skilled player requires a specific set of talents, while being a great coach requires a unique skill set that goes beyond just playing the game.

There are Hall of Fame coaches and players across all sports. However, being a great player does not always equate to being a great leader. Just because you are skilled, gifted, or tal-ented at completing a particular task does not mean you possess the qualities needed to lead others to accomplish the same task. It is not uncommon for someone to be an excellent salesperson, for instance, but struggle when promoted to a sales management position. Similarly, a great marketer might struggle when promoted to a marketing executive role, or an operations expert might falter as a CEO. This is because, in many cases, people are gifted and skilled at the task at hand but not in leadership.

On the other hand, some people may not excel in specific roles, such as sales, marketing, or operations, but are naturally gifted leaders who can successfully rally teams to achieve great results. These individuals are often referred to as Hall of Fame coaches. Their unique combination of skills, talents, and personality lends itself to effective leadership.

Unfortunately, many people who get promoted into leadership positions do not always pan out to be great leaders. The typical progression is from an entry-level position to middle management, and then to executive management and/or leadership. However, people often fail to evaluate whether a person is a great leader before promoting them. Just because someone excels in their current role does not necessarily mean they will be successful as a leader.

Therefore, it is essential to take a step back and evaluate your own strengths and weaknesses. Understand what works for you and do not feel pressured to follow a particular career path if it is not how you are wired. If you are gifted as a player, be the best player you can be. On the other hand, if you are not the best player, do not get discouraged because maybe there is something about you that would translate into effective leadership, and you could be a Hall of Fame coach.

It is all about the authentic journey you are on. Be true to yourself and your strengths. Look in the mirror and think about what is important to you. Understand where your heart and mind are and make decisions that align with that. If you try to force yourself into a role that does not suit you, you may miss out on opportunities to have a positive impact on those around you.

In conclusion, being a Hall of Fame player and being a Hall of Fame coach are two distinct paths in sports. While some people may excel in both roles, it is rare. It is essential to understand your own strengths and weaknesses and to be true to yourself when deciding which path to take. Do not feel pressured to follow a particular career path if it is not right for you. Instead, focus on what you are naturally gifted at, and strive to be the best you can be in that role.

MAKE THIS LAW PRACTICAL

Have I historically excelled more in completing tasks at a high level or in leading others to do so? Am I more suited to be a Hall of Fame Player like Michael Jordan or a Hall of Fame Coach like Phil Jackson?

19ᵀᴴ LAW

DON'T SHINE ON YOUR HATERS, MAKE YOUR HELPERS SHINE

IN THIS CHAPTER, we'll delve into the concept of focusing our attention and energy on the positive forces in our lives rather than getting caught up in negativity. It's easy to get bogged down by the haters and naysayers, but what we focus on grows. So instead of wasting time and energy trying to prove someone wrong or responding to their negativity, we should focus on the people who support us and help us shine.

The saying "shine on your haters" has become popular in recent years, but what does it really mean? It implies that we should ignore the negative comments and actions of others and continue to be our best selves, shining brightly despite their attempts to dim our light. While this can be a useful mindset in some situations, it also reinforces the idea that we should be focused on our detractors rather than our supporters.

The truth is, we will always have people in our lives who don't believe in us or actively try to bring us down. It's easy to get sucked into their negativity and spend our time and energy trying to prove them wrong. But this is a losing battle. No matter how hard we try, there will always be someone who doesn't like us or doesn't believe in us. And that's okay. We don't need everyone to be on our side to succeed.

What we do need, however, is to focus on the people who do support us. These are the people who believe in us, who encourage us, who amplify our message, and who are there for us when we need them. These are the people who help us shine.

When we focus on our helpers rather than our haters, we shift our energy in a positive direction. Instead of feeling discouraged by the negativity around us, we feel uplifted by the support of those who care about us. This helps us stay motivated and inspired to keep going, even when things get tough.

So how do we make our helpers shine? First and foremost, we need to acknowledge and appreciate them. We need to let them know how much we value their support and how much it means to us. This can be as simple as sending a thank-you note or message, or publicly acknowledging them on social media or in a speech.

We can also support our helpers in return. If someone has done something kind for us, we can find ways to repay the favor or pay it forward. We can also amplify their message or help them achieve their own goals. By supporting each other, we create a positive cycle of growth and success.

It's important to note that this doesn't mean we should ignore our haters completely. It's natural to feel hurt or frustrated when someone doesn't believe in us or actively tries to bring us down. But instead of dwelling on their negativity, we can use it as motivation to keep pushing forward and proving them wrong through our actions and achievements.

In conclusion, the concept of shining on our haters is well-intentioned but ultimately flawed. Instead of focusing on the negative forces in our lives, we should focus on the positive ones. By making our helpers shine brighter, we create a ripple effect of positivity and success that benefits us and those around us. So don't waste your energy on your haters. Focus on your helpers and watch yourself shine.

MAKE THIS LAW PRACTICAL

Whom do I feel the need to prove right in my life, and who are the people who have helped me and deserve public acknowledgment?

KEEP YOUR HANDS OFF THE WHEEL

THIS CHAPTER HIGHLIGHTS MY BELIEF IN THE POWER OF FAITH and staying in alignment with one's purpose. I believe that God created us with a unique purpose and that it is our responsibility to stay in communication with God to unlock that purpose. The analogy of "hands off the wheel and feet firmly placed on the gas and the brake" explains this thought process in relation to faith.

The phrase "hands off the wheel" represents the idea that a person allows the Holy Spirit to determine their direction. This means that they trust that there is a higher power guiding them and they are willing to surrender control to that power. I believe that by doing so, one is able to access their full potential and carry out their mission in full alignment with their unique purpose.

The second part of the analogy, "feet firmly placed on the gas and the brake", represents the importance of obedience to the guidance of the Holy Spirit. This means that I am willing to take action when I feel led to do so, and am also willing to stop or slow down when necessary. By staying obedient, I believe that I will be able to fully fulfill my purpose and stay on the path that God has intended for me.

I acknowledge that not everyone may share my beliefs in regards to faith. However, I hope that everyone can find inspiration in the idea of being guided by something much bigger than oneself. I encourage all readers to consider what it is that they are called to do in their specific moment, and to stay obedient to that calling.

In today's fast-paced world, it can be easy to get caught up in the constant busyness and demands of daily life. This message of faith and alignment serves as a reminder to take a step back and consider the bigger picture. By staying connected to a higher power and staying obedient to one's unique purpose, individuals can unlock their true potential and live a more fulfilling life.

In conclusion, the message in this chapter revolves around the power of faith and staying in alignment with one's purpose. My goal was to use the analogy of "hands off the wheel and feet firmly placed on the gas and the brake" to explain the importance of surrendering control to a higher power while also remaining obedient to one's unique purpose. While this message may not resonate with everyone, it serves as a reminder to stay connected to something bigger than oneself and to remain focused on fulfilling one's purpose in life.

MAKE THIS LAW PRACTICAL

What areas of my life should I submit to God to determine my direction, and am I obedient enough to act on spiritual guidance? If not, what is preventing me from doing so?

FULFILLMENT FOLLOWS FLOW

THE CONCEPT OF DOING WHAT YOU LOVE and never working a day in your life is a common mantra that has been around for many years. The idea is that if you find a job or activity that you are passionate about, it will feel less like work and more like a fulfilling experience. However, when we examine the definition of work, which is defined as force times distance, we can see that this concept doesn't entirely hold up.

Work is defined as the product of force and distance, where force is defined as pushing or pulling against something. So if we take out the force component of the equation, we are left with something that no longer is defined as work. This is where the idea of flow comes in. Flow is a state of mind where we are completely focused on a task or activity that we enjoy, to the point where we lose track of time and everything else around us.

The concept of flow was popularized by psychologist Mihaly Csikszentmihalyi, who identified it as a state of optimal experience.

When we are in a state of flow, we are completely focused on the task at hand, and we are not pushing or pulling against anything. Instead, we are allowing the task to flow through us. This is why flow can be seen as a substitute for force when it comes to the formula for work. Flow times distance is no longer work, but instead, it is a state of optimal experience.

However, it's important to note that flow doesn't happen automatically. It requires a certain level of skill and challenge in the activity or task, as well as a clear and immediate feedback loop. In other words, we need to have a sense of progress and accomplishment in order to enter a state of flow.

Moreover, the activity or task must align with our interests and passions. When we are engaged in an activity that we enjoy and are passionate about, we are more likely to enter a state of flow. This is why the concept of doing what you love and never working a day in your life can still hold some truth, even when we examine the definition of work.

Ultimately, the key to entering a state of flow is focus. As Steven Kotler puts it, "Flow follows focus." We need to be completely focused on the task at hand in order to enter a state of flow. This means eliminating distractions and allowing ourselves to fully immerse in the activity or task.

In conclusion, the concept of doing what you love and never working a day in your life can hold true if we substitute force with flow. When we are engaged in an activity that we are passionate about and allows us to enter a state of flow, it no longer feels like work. However, entering a state of flow requires a certain level of skill and challenge in the activity or task, as well as alignment with our interests and passions. Ultimately, the key to entering a state of flow is focus.

MAKE THIS LAW PRACTICAL

What am I pushing or pulling against (Force) that I need to release and replace with intense focus (Flow)?

22ᴺᴰ LAW

YOU DIDN'T FAIL, YOU FELL

HAVE YOU EVER EXPERIENCED FAILURE? That sinking feeling in your chest when you realize that despite your best efforts, things just didn't work out the way you planned. It's a feeling that can be hard to shake off and can often leave you feeling defeated and discouraged.

But what if I told you that failure isn't what you think it is? That the word itself is misleading, and that what you perceive as failure is just a temporary setback on your journey to success.

Let me explain. The word "fail" has a connotation of finality. When you fail at something, it's like a door slamming shut in your face, with no hope of ever opening again. But that's not really true, is it? The reality is that failure is rarely permanent. In fact, most successful people will tell you that they failed many times before they finally achieved their goals.

So why do we put so much weight on the concept of failure? Why do we allow ourselves to be defined by a single misstep or setback? Perhaps it's because we've been conditioned to believe that success is all about getting things right on the first try, that any deviation from that path is a sign of weakness or incompetence.

But that's a flawed way of thinking. The truth is that success is rarely a straight line. It's more like a zigzag, with plenty of ups and downs along the way. And if you're not prepared to weather those ups and downs, you're never going to get very far.

So, what can we do to shift our mindset around failure? Well, for starters, we can reframe the way we think about it. Instead of seeing failure as a dead end, we can view it as a detour or a speed bump. Something that slows us down temporarily, but doesn't stop us from reaching our destination.

And when we do encounter those setbacks, we can remind ourselves that they're not a reflection of our worth or abilities. They're simply part of the learning process. Every time we fall, we have an opportunity to get back up, dust ourselves off, and try again. And with each attempt, we get a little bit closer to where we want to be.

Of course, this is easier said than done. It's hard to let go of the fear of failure, especially when it feels like so much is at stake. But the truth is that the only way to truly succeed is to embrace the possibility of failure. To accept that it's going to happen, and to learn from it when it does.

So, if you're struggling with the fear of failure, here are a few things to keep in mind:

Failure is not final: As I mentioned earlier, failure is rarely permanent. It's just a temporary setback on the road to success. So don't let it define you or your abilities.

Failure is not a reflection of your worth: Just because you failed at something doesn't mean you're a failure as a person. It's important to separate your self-worth from your achievements.

Failure is a learning opportunity: Every time you fail, you have a chance to learn something new. Whether it's about yourself, your approach, or the task at hand, there's always something to take away from the experience.

Failure can be a steppingstone to success: Many successful people have failed multiple times before achieving their goals. In fact, some would argue that failure is a necessary step on the path to success.

Failure is not something to be ashamed of: Finally, it's important to remember that failure is a natural part of the learning process. It's nothing to be ashamed of or embarrassed about. Instead, embrace it as an opportunity to grow and improve. You didn't fail, you simply fell. Just like when you fell off of your bike as a kid, you now have the opportunity to get up.

MAKE THIS LAW PRACTICAL

Can you think of a situation that you perceived as a failure in the past, but you survived it and are still holding onto it? What would it take for you to reframe that experience from a "failure" to a "fall" and give yourself the ability to "get up" and move forward from it?

DOUBLE-DOWN ON YOU

IN EARLIER PODCAST EPISODES THAT I HOSTED, I referred to myself as Mr. Double Down on You. I created the Double Down on You Protocol, a coaching methodology that helps individuals navigate through life by embracing their greatness, pursuing their interests, recognizing their faults and failures, and guarding themselves against personal triggers. GIFT is an acronym for greatness, interest, faults and failures, and triggers.

Greatness is a concept that I believe everyone possesses. It can be a natural talent or a skill that one has learned over time. Regardless of its form, everyone has greatness in them. The key is to identify it. The next step is to identify one's interests. Everyone has something they are passionate about, something they enjoy doing in their free time. When one can find the intersectionality between their greatness and interests, they have unlimited potential. Professional athletes and entertainers are examples of individuals who have found their intersection and leveraged it to become the best in their field.

However, the path to success is not always smooth. In my coaching I stress the importance of recognizing one's faults and failures. Owning up to one's mistakes is crucial to moving forward. By acknowledging our faults and failures, we remove the leverage from those who may use them against us. Eminem's **last battle rap** scene in the movie "8 Mile" serves as an excellent example of taking ownership and removing the power from others who may try to use our negative components against us.

Lastly, I encourage everyone to prioritize the importance of recognizing our triggers. We all have them, and they can cause us to react in ways that are not beneficial. Identifying our triggers allows us to create a response to keep our emotions in check in challenging circumstances.

By unwrapping our unique gift, we can maximize our impact and fulfill our potential. The Double Down on You Protocol encourages individuals to embrace their greatness, pursue their interests, recognize their faults and failures, and guard themselves against their triggers. When we can do all of these things, we can double down on ourselves and achieve our dreams.

MAKE THIS LAW PRACTICAL

What is your personal G.I.F.T. that needs to be unwrapped?

Consider your greatness, interests, faults, and triggers.

24TH LAW

EMOTIONS ARE GREAT PASSENGERS AND HORRIBLE DRIVERS

EMOTIONS ARE AN INTEGRAL PART OF BEING HUMAN. They allow us to experience life's highs and lows, and they can provide valuable insight into our mental and physical well-being. However, it's crucial to recognize that emotions should not be the driver of our lives. Rather, emotions should serve as indicators, warning signs, and passengers in our metaphorical "car" of life.

The four primary emotions that we all experience are happiness, sadness, fear, and anger. Each emotion serves a specific purpose, and it's important to understand the role that they play in our lives. Happiness is an emotion that indicates we are content and fulfilled, while sadness can indicate that we are experiencing loss or grief. Fear can indicate that we are in danger, and anger can indicate that we feel threatened or wronged.

The key to managing our emotions effectively is to recognize that they should be passengers in our "car" of life, not the driver. When emotions are the driver, we are vulnerable to making decisions based on irrational and illogical thinking. This can lead to poor decision-making, damaged relationships, and negative outcomes.

Just as we want our passengers to be comfortable in our car, we should strive to ensure that our emotions are managed in a way that supports our overall well-being. This means taking steps to understand and process our emotions, rather than allowing them to dictate our actions.

There are several techniques that we can use to manage our emotions effectively. One effective strategy is to practice mindfulness, which involves paying attention to our thoughts, feelings, and bodily sensations without judgment. By becoming more aware of our emotions, we can learn to manage them more effectively and avoid getting caught up in unproductive or destructive patterns.

Another useful technique is cognitive restructuring, which involves challenging and changing negative thought patterns that can contribute to negative emotions. This can help us to develop more positive and productive ways of thinking and reacting, leading to better outcomes and improved overall well-being.

In addition to these techniques, it's essential to develop healthy coping strategies for managing stress and difficult emotions. This can involve things like exercise, meditation, deep breathing, or talking to a therapist or trusted friend. By taking proactive steps to manage our emotions and build resilience, we can enhance our ability to cope with life's challenges and achieve greater fulfillment and happiness.

In conclusion, emotions are a crucial part of being human, but they should not be the driver of our lives. Instead, emotions should serve as indicators and passengers in our metaphorical "car" of life. By managing our emotions effectively and developing healthy coping strategies, we can enhance our well-being, achieve our goals, and lead fulfilling lives. Remember, emotions can ride shotgun, but they should never drive the car.

MAKE THIS LAW PRACTICAL

Which emotions have I found the most challenging to control? Why do I think that is the case? Would seeking the help of a therapist to unpack my emotional baggage be a wise decision? Why or why not?

TREASURE THE DISCRETIONARY MOMENTS

WHEN WE HEAR THE TERM "DISCRETIONARY INCOME", we think of money that we can spend on anything we want. It's the leftover money we have after we've paid all our bills and expenses. But have you ever thought about discretionary time? The time we have that isn't spent on work, household chores, or other obligations. What do you do with that time?

Our discretionary moments are a window into who we are. If we have a day with no responsibilities, what do we choose to do? Do we spend hours scrolling through social media or binge-watching our favorite TV show? Or do we use that time to pursue hobbies, learn new skills, or connect with loved ones?

Just like with discretionary income, it's important to pay attention to where we spend our discretionary time. Do we spend it in ways that align with our values and goals? Or do we waste it on things that don't really matter?

If we want to maximize our impact and fulfillment in life, we need to be intentional with our discretionary moments. We need to make sure we're spending that time in ways that bring us joy, fulfillment, and growth.

So, take an inventory of your discretionary moments. Are there things you need to change? Maybe you need to set aside time for self-care or to pursue a passion project. Or maybe you need to be more intentional about how you spend time with loved ones.

By taking control of our discretionary moments, we can create a life that is more aligned with who we are and what we want to achieve. So, make the necessary changes and build upon the components that drive you. Remember, your discretionary moments are valuable, use them wisely.

MAKE THIS LAW PRACTICAL

Create a comprehensive list of how I typically spend my free time, including any discretionary moments. If this were to be my last moment on earth, would I feel ashamed of anything on that list? If so, why do I continue to spend my discretionary moments that way?

ACTION ALLEVIATES ANXIOUSNESS

ANXIETY, ANTICIPATION, AND ANXIOUSNESS are all common feelings that many individuals experience when thinking about creating or doing something. These feelings can be overwhelming and can prevent people from taking the necessary steps to achieve their goals. However, taking action is the key to overcoming these feelings and achieving success.

When we worry about things that have not happened yet, we tend to create negative scenarios in our minds that can cause anxiety and anticipation. However, once we start acting towards our goals, we often realize that the things we were worried about were not as significant as we thought they were. This is why taking action is so important.

As we embark on our journey to maximize our impact and optimize our fulfillment in life, we need to remember the importance of taking action. We must be willing to take the necessary steps to achieve our goals, even if it means facing our fears and anxieties head-on. By taking action, we can gain a better understanding of our abilities, limitations, and the things that truly matter to us.

When we take action, we are making a conscious decision to move forward towards our goals. We are no longer allowing our fears and anxieties to hold us back. Instead, we are choosing to take control of our lives and create the future we want for ourselves.

It's important to remember that taking action doesn't necessarily mean taking huge, dramatic steps towards our goals. It can be as simple as making a phone call, sending an email, or doing some research. The key is to take consistent and deliberate steps towards our goals, no matter how small they may be.

One way to think about taking action is to consider the concept of "definite no" versus "could have been yes." When we fail to take action, we are essentially choosing a "definite no" for ourselves. We are choosing to miss out on opportunities and experiences that could have been positive and fulfilling for us. On the other hand, when we take action, we are creating the possibility of a "could have been yes." We are opening ourselves up to new opportunities and experiences that could have a positive impact on our lives.

Taking action is like jumping into a cold swimming pool. It may be uncomfortable at first, but once we take that first step, we quickly adjust to the situation and realize that it's not as bad as we thought it would be. Similarly, once we start taking action towards our goals, we will begin to feel more confident and empowered, and our fears and anxieties will start to fade away.

Of course, it's important to acknowledge that some individuals may have clinical diagnoses of anxiety that require professional help. If you have been diagnosed with an anxiety disorder, it's important to speak with your healthcare provider about the appropriate treatment options.

For everyone else, however, taking action is a powerful tool for overcoming anxiety, anticipation, and anxiousness. By taking action, we can move past our fears and doubts and start creating the life we want for ourselves. It's important to remember that taking action is not always easy, but it is always worth it. So if you're feeling anxious or overwhelmed about a particular goal or project, remember to take action, even if it's just a small step in the right direction. With each step you take, you'll become closer to achieving your goals and living a fulfilling life.

MAKE THIS LAW PRACTICAL

Create a list of the things that are currently causing you the most anxiousness. What are some immediate actions you could take to reduce your anxiousness and address the items on your list?

COMMON VALUES SUPERSEDE DIFFERENT INTERESTS

ALIGNMENT MEANS THINGS WORKING WELL TOGETHER. People have different interests, but it's important to have common values for a strong connection. For example, my wife and I have different interests, but we share common values like our faith, goals, and values about money and raising kids. When building relationships, it's important to think about common values and not just shared interests. If you don't share common values, it's important to evaluate the relationship and decide if it's worth moving forward with.

Alignment is an essential element in creating a strong connection. It implies things working well together and being in order. In any relationship, whether it's a friendship or a romantic partnership, alignment is crucial. It allows for two people to be on the same page, to have a clear understanding of each other's wants and needs, and to work towards common goals.

In any relationship, individuals will have different interests. It's impossible for two people to have identical interests and be interested in the same things all the time. However, it's vital to have common values for a strong connection. Values are the foundation of any healthy relationship, and they provide a framework for understanding each other's motivations, decisions, and behaviors.

For example, I am married to my beautiful wife, Myisha, whom I love with all my heart. We have been together for several years, and over that time, we have developed different interests. I enjoy spending time listening to podcasts and watching sports, while she prefers mystery novels and watching crime drama TV shows. While we may not share the same interests, we have common values that align us.

Our faith is a central part of our lives, and we share the same values when it comes to our religious beliefs. We have long-term goals and missions that we work towards together, such as raising our children with love, empathy, and kindness. We have the same values when it comes to money and wealth, which means we are aligned in our spending habits and financial goals. These common values help us stay connected and work together, even when we have different interests.

When building relationships, it's essential to think about common values and not just shared interests. Interests can change over time, but values tend to remain constant. Values are the bedrock of any relationship, and they are what keep people connected, even when they don't always see eye to eye.

It's important to note that not all relationships will have common values, and that's okay. When you realize that you don't share common values with someone, it's crucial to evaluate the relationship and decide if it's worth moving forward with. Sometimes, people can have a great time together and share similar interests, but if their values are not aligned, the relationship may not be sustainable in the long term.

In conclusion, alignment is a crucial aspect of any relationship. It means that things are working well together and that two people are on the same page. While individuals will have different interests, it's vital to have common values for a strong connection. Values provide a framework for understanding each other's motivations, decisions, and behaviors. When building relationships, it's crucial to think about common values and not just shared interests. If you don't share common values, it's essential to evaluate the relationship and decide if it's worth moving forward with. Ultimately, a strong connection built on alignment and shared values can lead to a fulfilling and impactful life.

MAKE THIS LAW PRACTICAL

List the values that you share with your spouse, partners, teams, and community. Make a point to openly discuss these values on a regular basis.

GROWING UP IS A JOURNEY

BECOMING AN ADULT is a significant milestone in life. It means taking on responsibilities and being able to do what's necessary in the moment. It's a journey that both men and women take to become fulfilled and successful individuals. This journey requires maturity, self-awareness, and the willingness to do what needs to be done.

Being an adult means being able to make decisions and take actions that have consequences. It means being accountable for our actions and taking responsibility for our lives. When we focus on doing what's necessary in the moment, we can change the direction of our lives. It's not always easy, but it's necessary for growth and development. As we navigate through life, we gain skills and experiences that help us increase our capacity. We face challenges that test our willpower and teach us valuable lessons.

It's important to understand that being an adult is not a destination, but a journey. It's a continuous process of growth and development. It's not just about reaching a certain age or achieving certain milestones. It's about the choices we make and the actions we take in our everyday lives. Every day presents an opportunity to learn, grow, and become better versions of ourselves.

One of the key aspects of being an adult is the ability to take care of oneself. This means taking care of our physical, mental, and emotional well-being. It means developing healthy habits that will help us live long, happy, and fulfilling lives. Self-care is not a selfish act, but rather a necessary one. When we take care of ourselves, we are better able to take care of those around us.

Another important aspect of being an adult is the ability to contribute to society. As we develop our skills and capacities, we are better equipped to make a positive impact in the world. This can be through our work, our relationships, or our volunteer activities. When we all do our part, society benefits.

It's important to note that becoming an adult is not always easy. It requires effort, perseverance, and a willingness to face our fears and overcome our challenges. However, the rewards of becoming a successful and fulfilled adult are immeasurable. We can have meaningful relationships, a fulfilling career, and a sense of purpose and belonging.

In conclusion, being an adult is a journey that requires maturity, self-awareness, and the willingness to do what needs to be done. It means taking care of ourselves and contributing to society. It's a continuous process of growth and development, and every day presents an opportunity to learn and become better versions of ourselves. If we all do our part, society can benefit from our contributions.

MAKE THIS LAW PRACTICAL

What phase of your personal growth journey do you feel you are currently in?

29TH LAW

CONQUER THE MOMENT

WHEN ASKED HOW THINGS ARE GOING IN PUBLIC, I often respond with "one moment at a time, no faster, no slower." Unfortunately, some people automatically assume that something negative is happening in my life when I say this. But the truth is that focusing on the present moment is the key to a fulfilling life.

We cannot control the past or the future, but we do have control over the present moment. The decisions we make in each moment determine the direction of our lives. To conquer each moment, we need either confidence or courage. Confidence is rooted in our experiences, while courage is rooted in our belief systems.

If we want to strengthen our confidence, we need to build up our bank of experiences. This means doing things and taking risks. If we want to strengthen our courage, we need to test our current belief systems and work on developing a mindset that supports our goals.

Conquering each moment requires making contributions to both our bank of confidence and our bank of courage. By doing so, we can live more present lives, make sound decisions, and operate from a place of authenticity. This leads to a greater sense of fulfillment and maximizes our impact on society.

Impact is simply the difference between our involvement and our potential involvement in a situation. By focusing on the present moment and conquering each moment with confidence or courage, we can maximize our impact and make a positive difference in the world.

The concept of living one moment at a time is often associated with addiction recovery programs. In these programs, individuals are encouraged to focus on staying sober for just one day at a time. The same principle can be applied to everyday life. Instead of worrying about the past or the future, we can focus on the present moment and make the most of it.

This approach requires mindfulness and a willingness to let go of past regrets and future worries. It also requires a belief in our own ability to handle whatever challenges may arise in the moment.

To build confidence, we can look to our past successes and accomplishments. We can also challenge ourselves to try new things and take risks. By stepping outside of our comfort zone, we can build up our resilience and our ability to handle challenges.

Building courage requires a willingness to challenge our own beliefs and assumptions. We must be open to the possibility that we may be wrong or that our beliefs may not serve us well. This requires a certain level of humility and a willingness to learn and grow. We all must be willing to ask ourselves four questions regarding our beliefs: What do I believe? Why do I believe it? How am I practicing or reinforcing this belief? How am I putting this belief to the test?

When we focus on conquering each moment, we are better able to live in the present and make the most of our lives. We can approach each day with a sense of purpose and direction, knowing that our actions in each moment will determine the direction of our lives.

Living one moment at a time does not mean that we ignore the past or fail to plan for the future. Rather, it means that we recognize that the present moment is the only moment we have control over. By making the most of each moment, we can create a life that is fulfilling and meaningful.

In conclusion, conquering each moment with confidence or courage is a key to a fulfilling life. By focusing on the present moment, we can make sound decisions, live authentically, and maximize our impact on society. This approach requires mindfulness, a willingness to let go of the past and future, and a belief in our own ability to handle whatever challenges may arise.

MAKE THIS LAW PRACTICAL

Create a comprehensive list of my experiences, lessons learned, and accomplishments. These components will form my "bank of confidence." Identify and list my core beliefs or belief systems. Then, for each belief, answer the following four questions: What do I believe? Why do I believe it? How do I regularly practice or reinforce this belief? How have I put this belief to the test? The beliefs will form my "bank of courage." Periodically draw from both my bank of confidence and my bank of courage to help me tackle challenging situations.

YOUR NETWORK IS NOT YOUR NET WORTH

IN TODAY'S SOCIETY, we are constantly bombarded with messages about the importance of networking. We're told that our network is our net worth, and that our success is dependent on the relationships we have built. While it's certainly true that having strong connections can be beneficial, I believe that there is a significant difference between a network and a community.

I was fortunate to have the opportunity to interview Dr. Vibe, a dynamic brother from Toronto, and we had a deep conversation about the distinction between a community and a network. During our discussion, we explored the idea that a network is a group of entities that are connected only when someone is in need of the other. In contrast, a community is a collective group that has a vested interest in the whole entity succeeding. When people contribute to a community, they do so not just for their personal benefit, but for the benefit of the collective.

The concept of networking has become so prevalent in our culture that we often forget the importance of building a community. We're taught to focus solely on what we can get out of a relationship, rather than investing in the collective growth, development, and good of the community. While networking may be useful in the short term, it's the community that will ultimately sustain us and help us thrive in the long term.

If we view our network as our net worth, we are placing our value in the hands of others. We become dependent on our connections and their perception of us, rather than our own intrinsic value. Our worth is no longer our own, but rather determined by the value of those entities we are connected to. This means that we can easily be used or viewed as a pass-through to the real value propositions of relationships.

Furthermore, relying solely on our network can be risky. What happens when our network is no longer available, or someone no longer needs us to connect them to the source they're ultimately trying to reach? If our worth is based solely on our network, we may find ourselves without a solid foundation to fall back on.

In contrast, when we prioritize building a community, we invest in the collective good. We contribute to something larger than ourselves, which can provide a sense of fulfillment and purpose. We no longer view relationships as transactions but as meaningful connections that can help us grow as individuals and as a community.

Building a community also means that we prioritize quality over quantity. While it's tempting to accumulate as many connections as possible, a community is built on deep, meaningful relationships. We need to focus on building genuine connections that are based on shared values, mutual respect, and a commitment to the community's growth and success.

In essence, the difference between a network and a community is the difference between a short-term strategy and a long-term vision. Building a network may help us achieve immediate goals, but building a community will sustain us and help us thrive in the long term. When we prioritize community, we build something that has the potential to last for generations, rather than just fleeting moments of success.

In conclusion, while networking certainly has its benefits, it's important to remember that our true value lies not in our network, but in the value we bring to the table. By prioritizing building a community over building a network, we invest in something larger than ourselves, and we create a foundation for sustained growth and success. We must remember that our connections are only as valuable as the meaning and depth we give to them, and that investing in a community is ultimately investing in ourselves.

MAKE THIS LAW PRACTICAL

Create a summary of your professional experience without mentioning any educational institutions, employers, businesses, or associations, and without mentioning your degrees, certifications, or credentials. The goal of this exercise is to focus on your actual experiences and competencies, rather than relying on credentials and connections to build value.

31ˢᵀ LAW

BUILD A ROCKET SHIP

IN OUR SOCIETY, it's easy to get caught up in the idea of chasing after stars - those individuals who seem to have it all, whether it be a large following on social media, a successful career, or the appearance of wealth and influence. We see them as gateways to success and believe that if we can just wrangle that one star, we'll finally be able to reach the promised land.

But the truth is, chasing after stars is a losing proposition. It's like trying to catch a shooting star - by the time you think you've caught it, it's already gone. And even if you do manage to catch that star, it's not a guarantee that it will lead you to success. In fact, more often than not, it's simply a distraction from the real work that needs to be done.

Instead of chasing after stars, I propose that we build rocket ships. What do I mean by that? I mean using the resources, tools, and relationships at our disposal to create something that can propel us to success. It's not about relying on one person or entity to take us to the next level - it's about taking matters into our own hands and creating something that is uniquely ours.

The beauty of building a rocket ship is that it's something that's entirely within our control. We don't have to wait for someone else to give us permission or opportunities - we can create them ourselves. And when we do that, we're no longer chasing after stars - we're among them.

Of course, building a rocket ship isn't always easy. It takes time, effort, and resources to create something that can truly propel us to success. But the good news is that we already have everything we need at our disposal. It's just a matter of recognizing the tools and relationships we have and putting them to use.

One of the biggest hurdles that many of us face when it comes to building our own rocket ships is our own self-doubt. We don't believe that we have what it takes to succeed, or that we have the resources necessary to make it happen. But the truth is, that kind of thinking is a self-fulfilling prophecy. If we don't believe in ourselves and our abilities, we'll never be able to create something that can truly propel us to success.

That's why it's so important to change our mindset and start believing that we have what it takes to build our own rocket ships.

We need to recognize that we already have the tools, resources, and relationships we need to make it happen - we just need to put them to use.

Building a rocket ship is all about taking control of our own destiny. It's about recognizing that we don't have to rely on anyone else to succeed - we have the power to create our own opportunities. And when we do that, we'll no longer be chasing after stars - we'll be among them, navigating as peers.

In conclusion, chasing after stars may seem like an attractive prospect, but it's ultimately a losing proposition. Instead of focusing on one individual or entity to lead us to success, we should focus on building our own rocket ships. By using the tools, resources, and relationships at our disposal, we can create something that can truly propel us to success. It's not always easy, but it's entirely within our control. And when we do succeed, we'll realize that we don't need the stars we were chasing to begin with. We'll be among them, navigating our own path to success.

MAKE THIS LAW PRACTICAL

What relationships, resources, and tools do I have available that could contribute to building my "Personal Rocket Ship"?

DON'T BECOME THE PEPPERCORN

THE CONCEPT OF "GRIND" has become increasingly popular in modern culture, particularly in the context of work and productivity. It's often associated with the idea of pushing oneself to the limit, working tirelessly towards a goal, and persevering through challenges. However, this approach can be problematic when it's not accompanied by a sense of purpose and direction. In other words, grinding for the sake of grinding can lead to burnout, disillusionment, and a sense of being stuck in a never-ending cycle of toil.

To better understand this phenomenon, let's consider the metaphor of grinding fresh peppercorns. When we grind peppercorns, we're exerting a significant amount of force to break down the tough outer layer and release the fragrant, flavorful inner core. This process can be satisfying and even enjoyable when we're using a high-quality grinder and fresh peppercorns. However, if the grinder is dull or the peppercorns are stale, the process can become tedious and frustrating.

Likewise, when we approach our work or personal goals with a sense of alignment and purpose, the act of "grinding" can feel invigorating and empowering. We're putting in effort towards something that we truly care about, and we can see the tangible results of our labor. On the other hand, when we're simply going through the motions, grinding away without any real sense of direction or fulfillment, the process can feel draining and meaningless.

So, how can we ensure that we're aligned with our purpose and avoiding the trap of mindless grinding? The first step is to get clear on what our unique and divine assignment is. This might involve reflecting on our values, strengths, passions, and sense of calling. It may also involve seeking guidance from mentors, coaches, or spiritual advisors who can help us discern our path.

Once we have a sense of our purpose, we can begin to take intentional action towards our goals. This might involve setting clear objectives, breaking them down into manageable steps, and establishing a regular practice of discipline and focus. It may also involve cultivating a sense of gratitude and mindfulness, acknowledging the progress that we're making and staying connected to our deeper motivations.

Ultimately, the key to avoiding the trap of grinding is to stay connected to our sense of purpose and to align our efforts with that purpose. When we're operating from a place of clarity and intentionality, the act of working towards our goals can be a source of joy, growth, and fulfillment. On the other hand, when we're grinding away without any sense of purpose or direction, we're likely to end up feeling depleted, frustrated, and disconnected from our deeper selves.

So, the next time someone tells you to "grind it out," ask yourself whether you're aligned with your purpose and whether the effort you're putting in is truly meaningful. If the answer is yes, then grind away with joy and determination. But if you're feeling like a peppercorn in the midst of a grinder, it may be time to step back, reassess, and realign your efforts with your unique and divine assignment.

MAKE THIS LAW PRACTICAL

Create a list of activities or affiliations that make you feel like you are being ground down, like a peppercorn in a grinder. Why are you staying in the grinder?

33RD LAW

ALWAYS TRUST YOUR A.S.S. (ALIGNMENT, SELF-MASTERY & SERVICE)

IN THE 90S, the popular Bell Biv DeVoe song "Poison" had a memorable line: "never trust a big butt and a smile." Similar to how battle rappers utilize the content of their competitor, I used this lyric as inspiration for a tongue-in-cheek response and creation of the acronym, "Always Trust Your A.S.S."

As a man of faith, I believe that everything good and perfect comes from above. In my belief, alignment, self-mastery, and service are essential to fulfilling our divine purpose. When we are aligned with our purpose, we are in proper order, and we are better able to create a positive ripple effect in the world. One particular movement, one specific adjustment, can have monumental effects when we are aligned properly. I believe that there is a bigger force at work in the world, which I refer to as the Holy

Spirit, and we must be obedient and aligned to have the proper impact we are destined to have.

In my journey, I have realized that God does not give us a 40-step plan. Instead, God gives us part of our plan as we are directly aligned with the purpose that he has placed in our heart, and soul. This unique setup allows us to stay in direct communication with our Creator and recognize whether or not we need to make adjustments. Alignment is extremely important because it enables us to achieve our unique purpose and create a positive impact in the world.

Once we understand our purpose, it is incumbent upon us to achieve self-mastery. Self-mastery requires us to put in the work to achieve mastery over our gifts, talents, and skills. It is our responsibility to master ourselves so that we can better serve others. It is important to understand the relationships we have in our community, the individuals we have access to, and the tools we have at our disposal.

Service is essential to putting our gift, talent, or skill to work. Whether we are in business, education, or nonprofit work, we are all in service to others. The purpose of our aligned talent, gift, and/or skill is to improve the lives of those we have access to. Service is vital to creating a positive impact in the world.

In conclusion, alignment, self-mastery, and service are the key pillars to fulfilling our divine purpose. When we are in alignment with our purpose, we are better able to achieve self-mastery, which allows us to serve others better. As **people** of faith, it is our responsibility to stay in direct communication with our Creator, recognize our unique purpose, and use our gifts, tal-ents, and skills in a service capacity to impact the world positively.

MAKE THIS LAW PRACTICAL

Do I feel that I am currently in alignment with my purpose? If not, why do I think that is the case? What daily actions do I take to pursue self-mastery? Make a list of ways that I can im-prove my service to others. Take immediate action to implement these changes.

FINAL LAW
(CONCLUSION)

In the world of track and field, the 400 meter world record for men is currently 43.03 seconds, while the world record for the men's 4x100 meter relay is 36.84 seconds. Surprisingly, despite being the same distance, the relay is run about six seconds faster than the individual race. The difference lies in the fact that in the relay, each team member passes the baton to someone else, making the overall process more efficient. This analogy is useful for understanding the importance of passing the baton in order to reach your goals more efficiently.

As we focus on becoming peak performers in leading from within, we must understand and utilize the relay race analogy. Trying to tackle everything on our own will slow us down, just like running the 400 meters without passing the baton. Instead, we need to understand our personal limits and capabilities and know what leg of the race we are responsible for running. Leading from within means recognizing that we are not designed to run the race alone. The six-second difference between the two track events is a clear indication of this.

If we want to maximize our impact and fulfillment, we need to become peak performers in leading from within. This requires us to understand the leg of the race we're responsible for and run that well, then pass the baton to the next person. As leaders, we must also think about our succession plan, even if we're just starting to lead from within. It's essential to consider who we'll pass the baton to, and this is a critical part of our legacy as leaders.

Understanding the relay race analogy is essential for maximizing our performance in leading from within. We must know our strengths and limitations and learn to work efficiently with others. By doing this, we can achieve our goals and leave a legacy as effective leaders.

In conclusion, the 33 laws of impact and fulfillment are not just a set of rules to be followed, but a way of life to be embraced. They are a reminder that we have the power to create our own impact and find fulfillment in our lives. While there is no external force requiring these laws, we have the responsibility to self-govern and choose to live within them. The journey towards impact and fulfillment is not always easy, but it is always worth it. So, go forth and be great. Make an impact, find fulfillment, and live the amazing life that you were meant to live.